PIANO · VOCAL · GUITAR

THE LUMINEERS III

ISBN: 978-1-5400-7017-3

Visit Hal Leonard Online at
www.halleonard.com

Contact us:
Hal Leonard
7777 West Bluemound Road
Milwaukee, WI 53213
Email: info@halleonard.com

In Europe, contact:
Hal Leonard Europe Limited
42 Wigmore Street
Marylebone, London, W1U 2RN
Email: info@halleonardeurope.com

In Australia, contact:
Hal Leonard Australia Pty. Ltd.
4 Lentara Court
Cheltenham, Victoria, 3192 Australia
Email: info@halleonard.com.au

DONNA

Words and Music by JEREMY FRAITES
and WESLEY SCHULTZ

Slowly

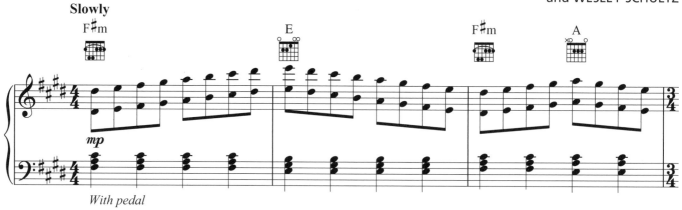

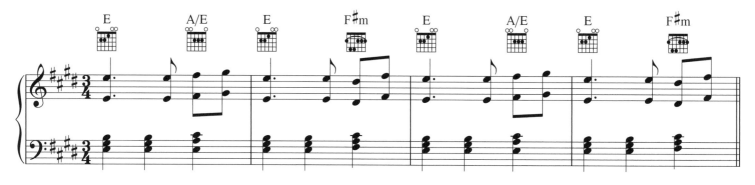

It's not the words you say, but how you say it. I saved a pic-ture where your hair was braid-ed.

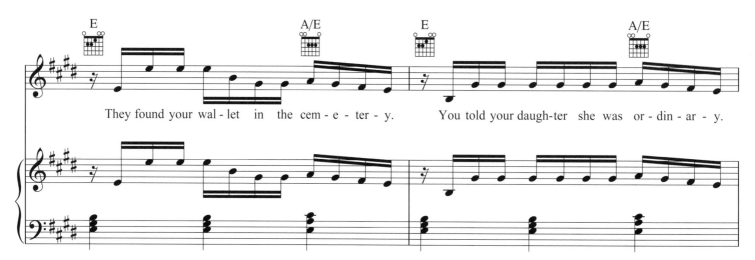

They found your wal-let in the cem-e-ter-y. You told your daugh-ter she was or-din-ar-y.

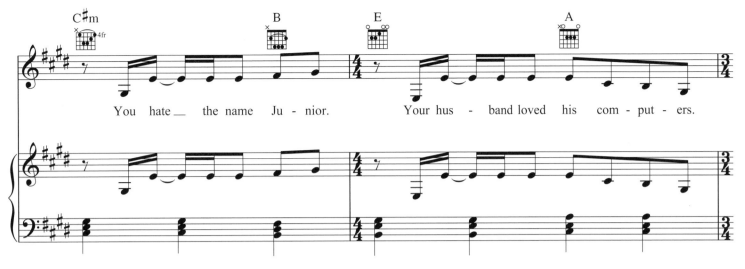

You hate ___ the name Ju - nior. Your hus - band loved his com - put - ers.

Your moth - er nev-er was one, the eld - est of sev - en chil-dren.

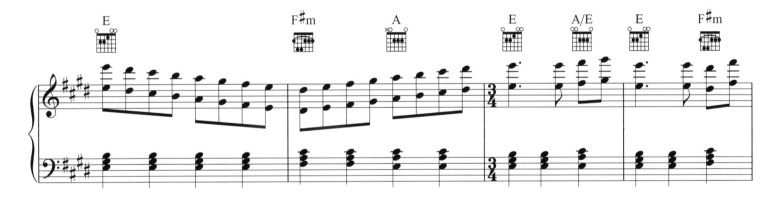

If you don't have it, then you'll nev - er give it. And I don't blame you for the way you're liv - ing.

A lit-tle boy was born in Feb-ru-ar-y. You could-n't so-ber up to hold a ba-by.

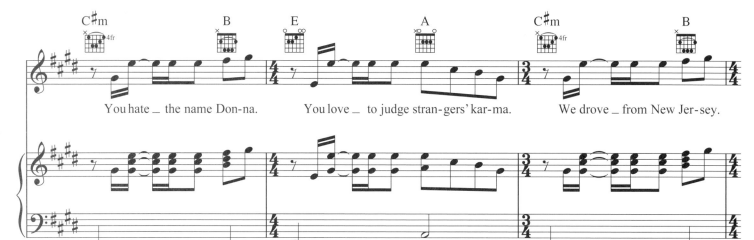

You hate __ the name Don-na. You love __ to judge stran-gers' kar-ma. We drove __ from New Jer-sey.

The trucks __ al-ways made you wor-ry. Oh, __ my hen-na tat-too,

go __ to bed, __ it's way __ too late.

5

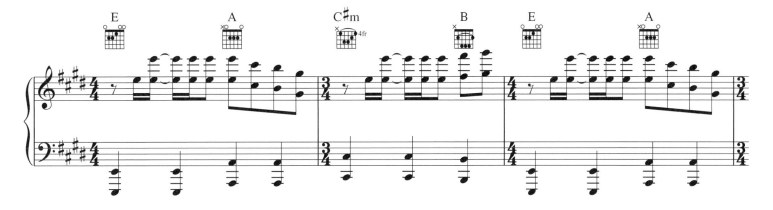

You hate __ the name Don-na.   You love __ to judge stran-gers' kar-ma.   You drove __ from New Jer-sey.

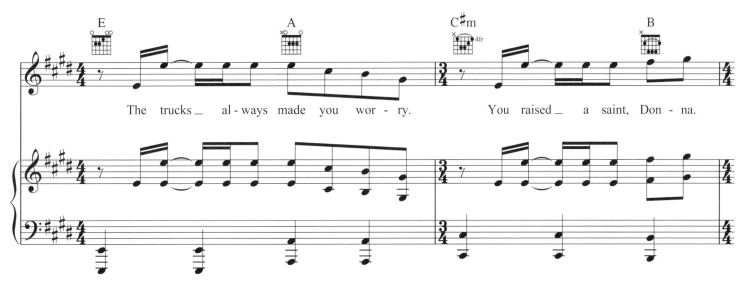

The trucks __ al-ways made you wor-ry.   You raised __ a saint, Don - na.

You loved __ to judge stran-gers' kar - ma.   You're pray - ing for a fu - ner - al.

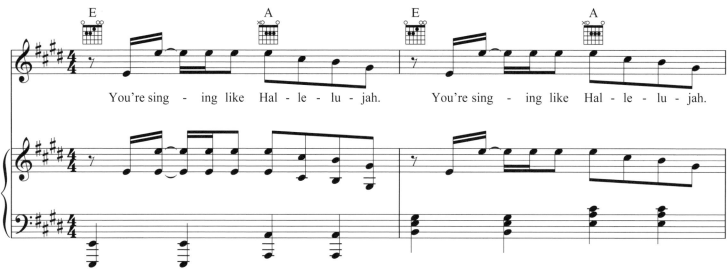

You're sing - ing like Hal - le - lu - jah. You're sing - ing like Hal - le - lu - jah.

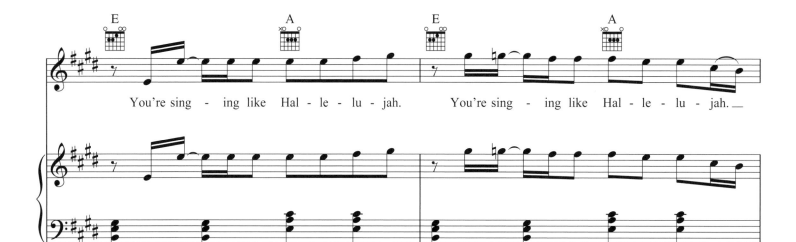

You're sing - ing like Hal - le - lu - jah. You're sing - ing like Hal - le - lu - jah.

You're sing - ing like Hal - le - lu - jah.

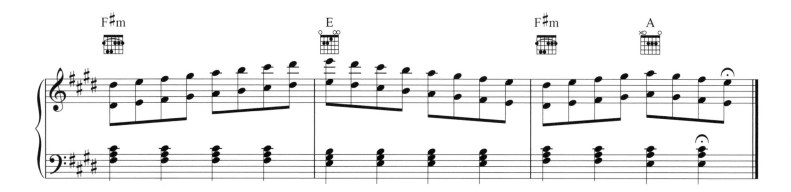

JIMMY SPARKS

Words and Music by JEREMY FRAITES
and WESLEY SCHULTZ

Slightly faster

Jim-my be-lieved in the A-mer-i-can way. ___ A pri-son guard, he worked hard
Jim-my loved Bon-nie and he fa-ther'd a kid. ___ A ba-by boy, but the moth-

and made the min-i-mum wage. He found his free-dom lock-in' men in a cage, __ oh. ____
er had oth-er reas-ons to live. She left the ba-by with a note on the bed, __ oh. ____

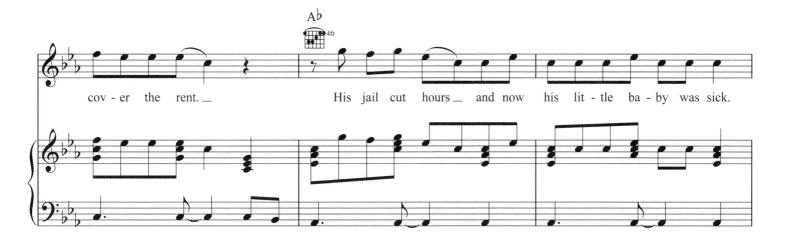

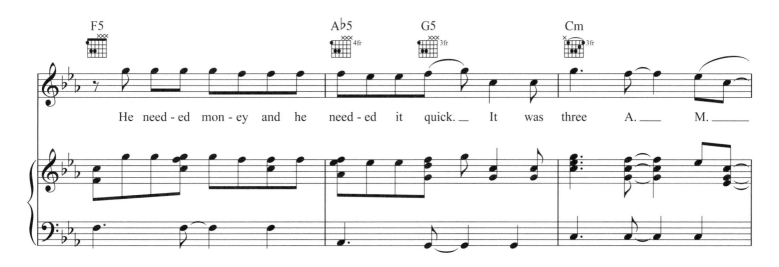

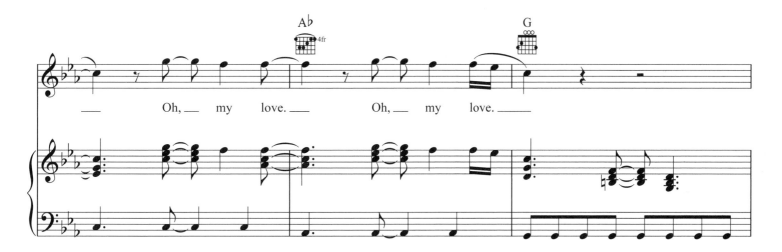

Could you spare __ my blood, __ spare __ my blood. __

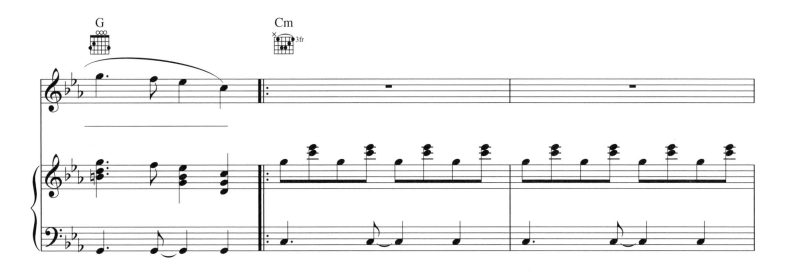

Jim woke his son and buck-led him in the car. __ They drove an hour __ from town
Af-ter an hour, __ Jim-my dou-bled his cash. __ He took his kid and his win-

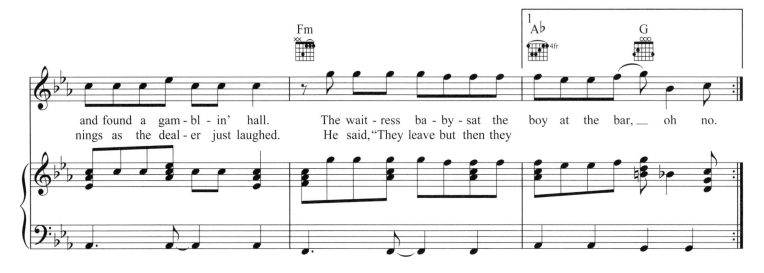

and found a gam-bl-in' hall. The wait-ress ba-by-sat the boy at the bar, __ oh no.
nings as the deal-er just laughed. He said, "They leave but then they

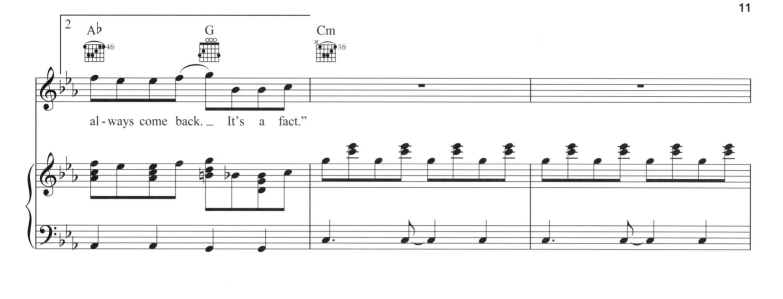

al-ways come back._ It's a fact."

Out on the road,_ they caught a stran - ger in the lights._ His thumb was up and his son

asked if the man was al-right. Jim said, "You nev - er give a hitch - er a ride_ 'cause it's

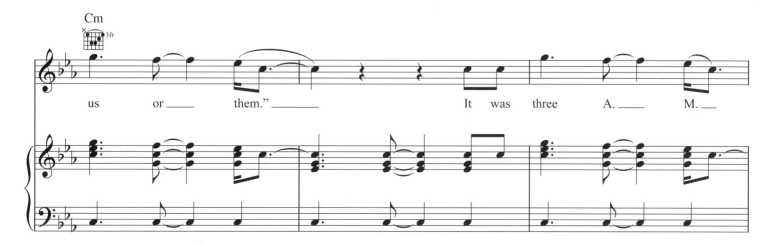

us or ___ them." ___ It was three A. ___ M. __

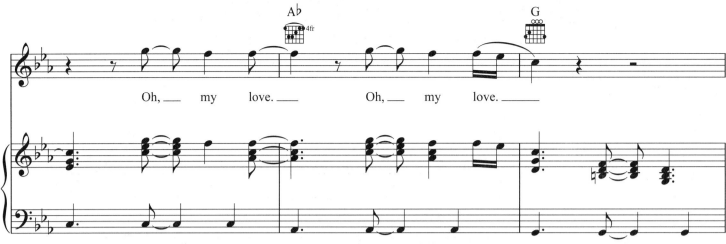

Oh, __ my love. __ Oh, __ my love. _____

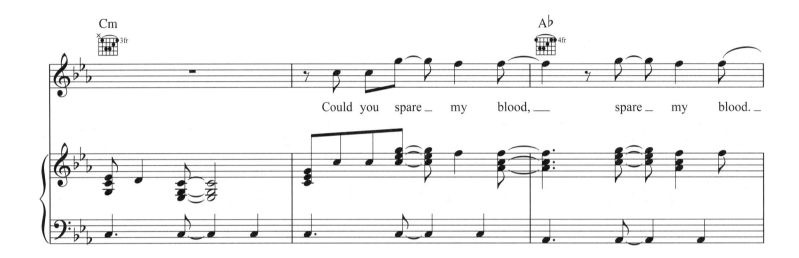

Could you spare __ my blood, __ spare __ my blood. __

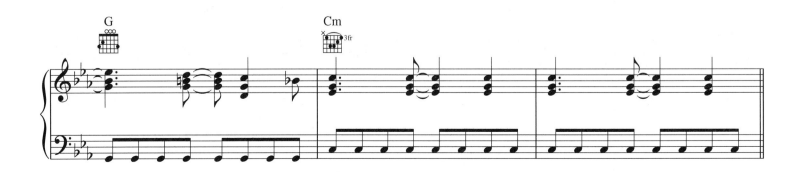

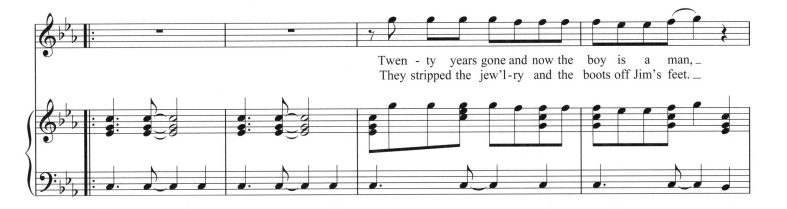

Twen - ty years gone and now the boy is a man, _
They stripped the jew'l-ry and the boots off Jim's feet. _

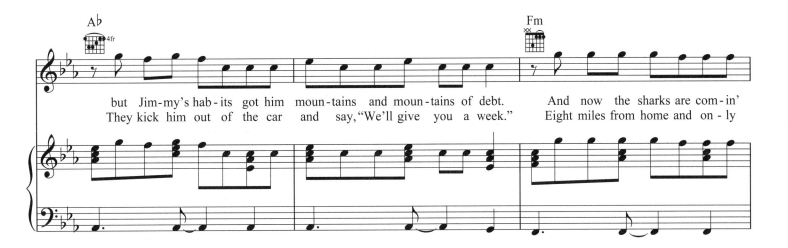

Ab   Fm

but Jim-my's hab-its got him moun-tains and moun-tains of debt.   And now the sharks are com-in'
They kick him out of the car   and say, "We'll give you a week."   Eight miles from home and on - ly

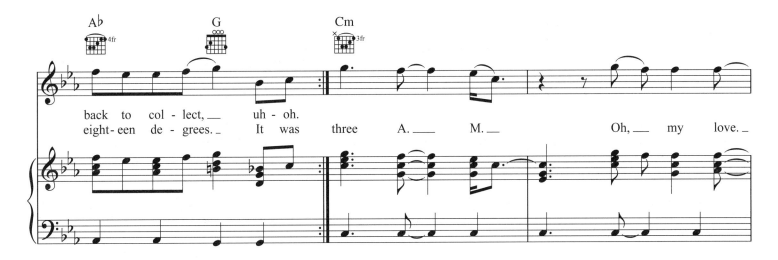

Ab   G   Cm

back to col - lect, _ uh - oh.   It was   three   A. _   M. _   Oh, _ my love. _
eight-een de - grees. _

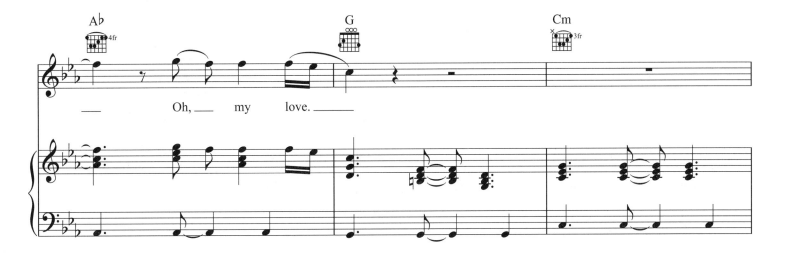

Ab   G   Cm

_   Oh, _ my   love. _____

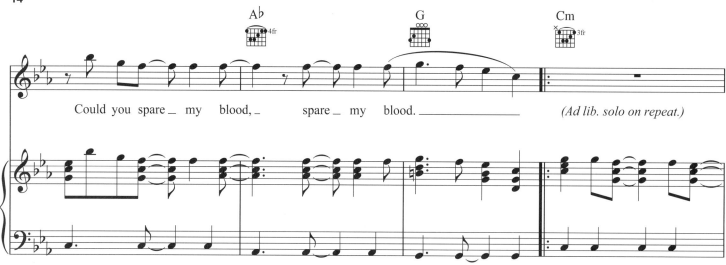

Could you spare __ my blood, __ spare __ my blood. _____ *(Ad lib. solo on repeat.)*

Slower

Now Jim-my's son is try'n a make his way home. __
His old man waved his hands with tears in his eyes __

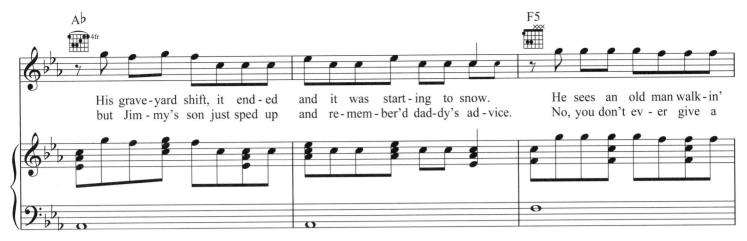

His grave-yard shift, it end-ed and it was start-ing to snow. He sees an old man walk-in'
but Jim-my's son just sped up and re-mem-ber'd dad-dy's ad-vice. No, you don't ev - er give a

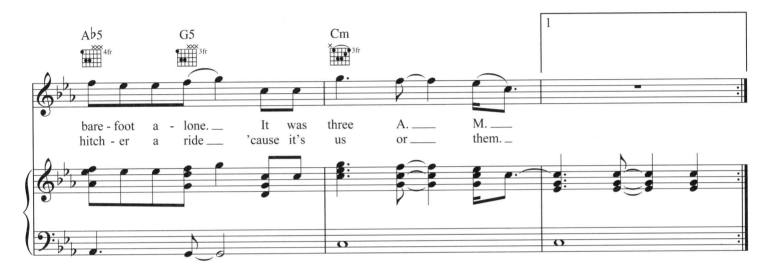

bare - foot a - lone. __ It was three A. __ M. __
hitch - er a ride __ 'cause it's us or __ them. __

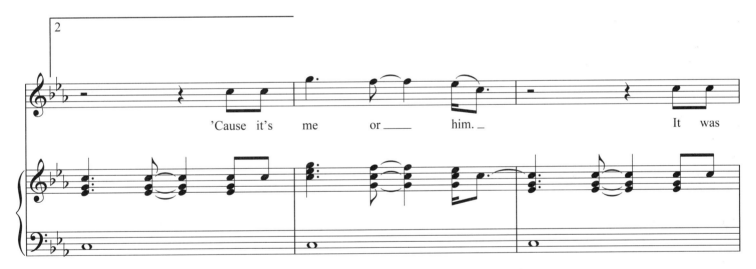

'Cause it's me or __ him. __ It was

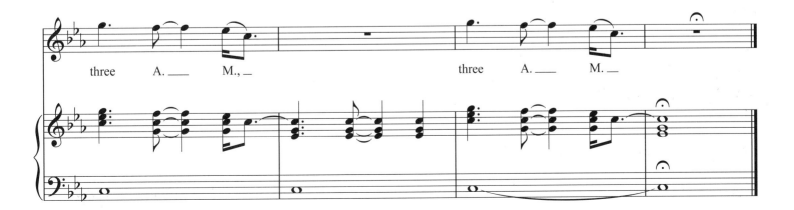

three A. __ M., __ three A. __ M. __

LIFE IN THE CITY

Words and Music by JEREMY FRAITES
and WESLEY SCHULTZ

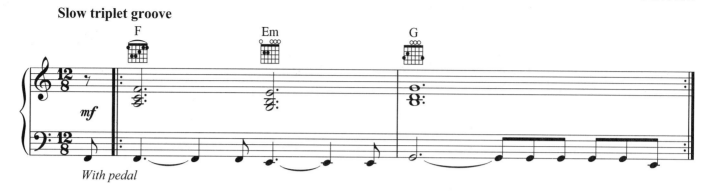

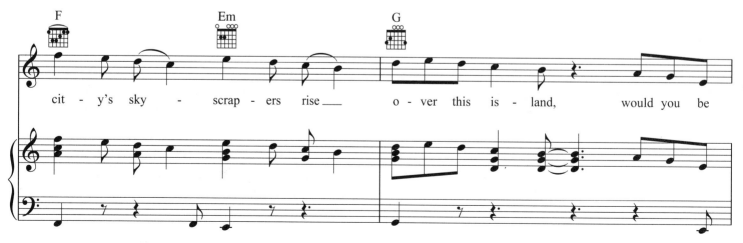

glad to see Man-hat-tan for once? ___ I knew the

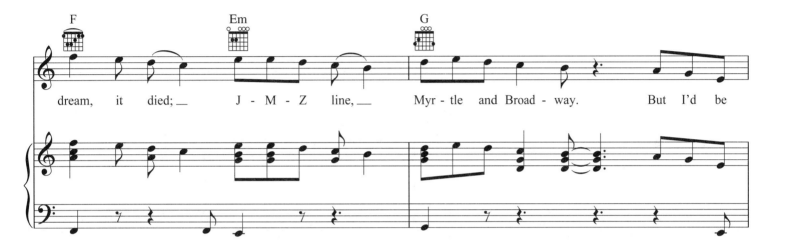

dream, it died; ___ J - M - Z line, ___ Myr - tle and Broad - way. But I'd be

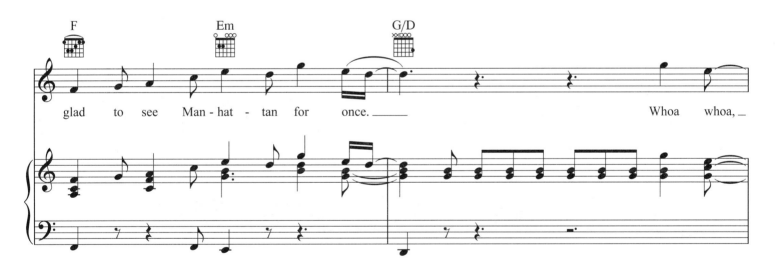

glad to see Man-hat-tan for once. ___ Whoa whoa, __

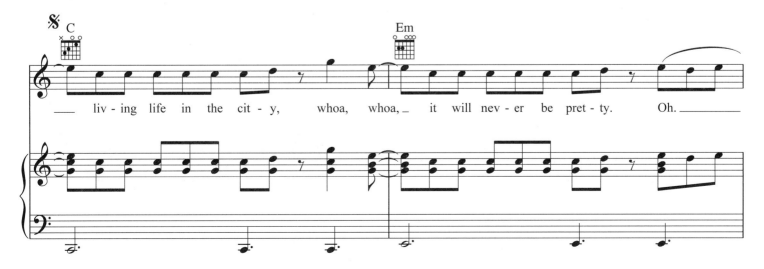

___ liv-ing life in the cit - y, whoa, whoa, __ it will nev - er be pret - ty. Oh. ___

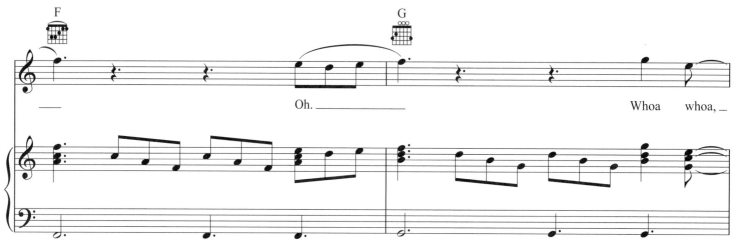

Oh. _____ Whoa whoa, ___

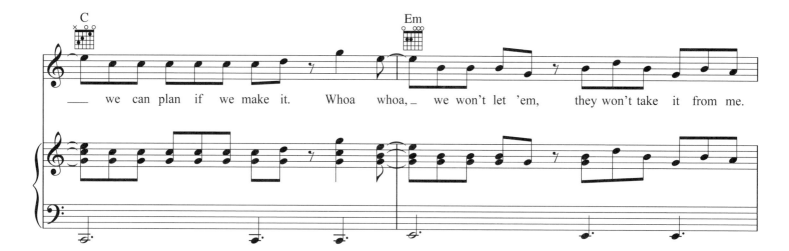

___ we can plan if we make it. Whoa whoa, ___ we won't let 'em, they won't take it from me.

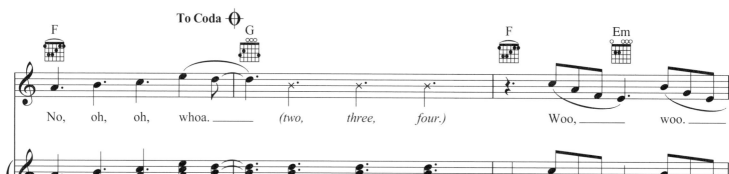

To Coda ⊕

No, oh, oh, whoa. _____ *(two, three, four.)* Woo, _____ woo. _____

Woo, _____ woo. _____

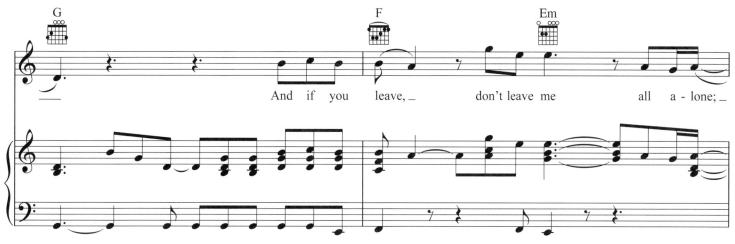

And if you leave, _ don't leave me all a-lone; _

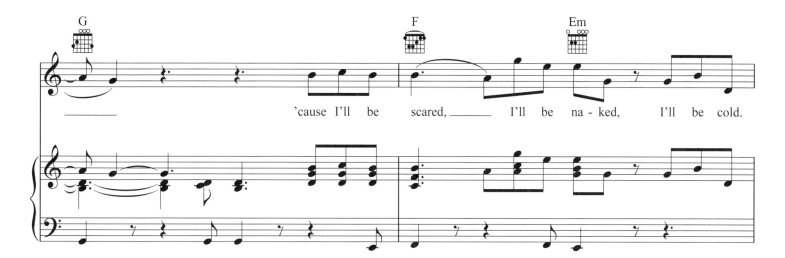

_____ 'cause I'll be scared, _____ I'll be na-ked, I'll be cold.

And I miss my dad _ and Cle-o-pat - ra

sit-ting on the phone. _ So take me back _____ off these _ streets, and we'll

never be a part, __ to - geth - er from the start, __

D.S. al Coda

nev - er, nev - er fall - ing back a - lone. __ Whoa __ whoa, __

CODA

And if the sun don't shine on me to - da
da da da _____ da da

day, and if the sub - ways flood and bridg - es
da. Da da da da da da _____ da ____ da

break,
da.

will you just lay _____ down and dig your
Da da da da _____ da da _____ da da

grave,
da.

or will you rail a - gainst your dy - ing
Da da da da _____ da da _____ da _____ da

day?

Da da da da _____ da da _____ da da

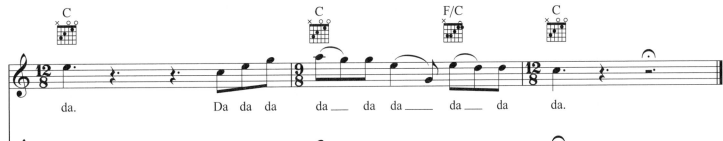

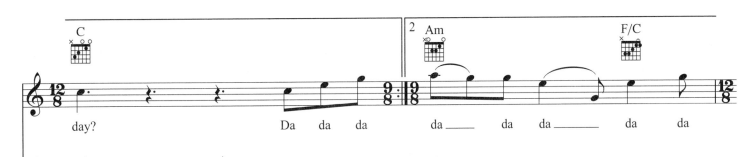

da.

Da da da da _____ da da _____ da _____ da da.

GLORIA

Words and Music by JEREMY FRAITES
and WESLEY SCHULTZ

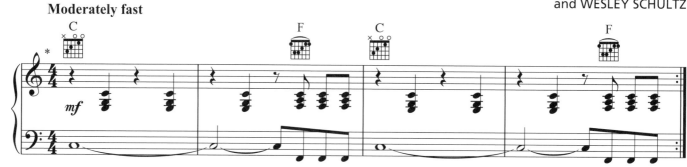

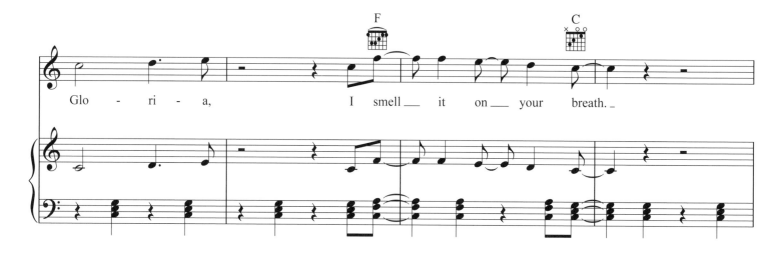

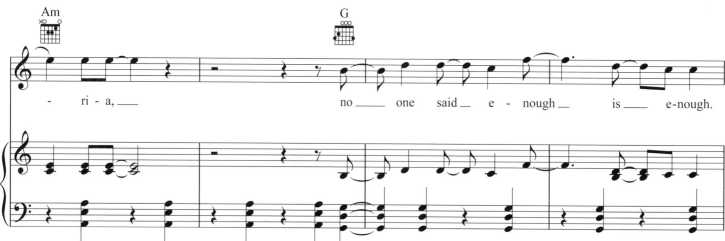

Glo - ri - a, I smell _ it on _ your breath. _

Glo - ri - a, booze _ and pep - per - mint. Glo -

- ri - a, _ no _ one said _ e - nough _ is _ e-nough.

Recorded a half step lower.

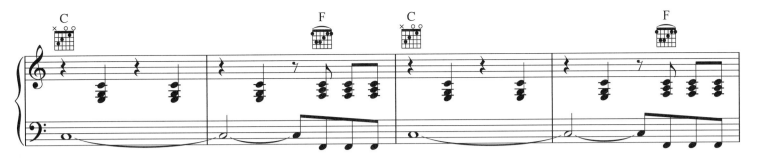

Glo - ri - a, they found you on the floor.

Glo - ri - a, my hand was tied to yours. Glo-

- ri - a, did you fi - n'lly see that e - nough is e - nough?

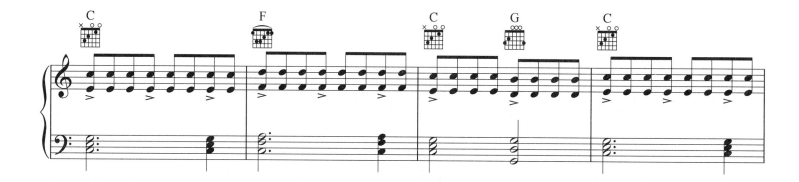

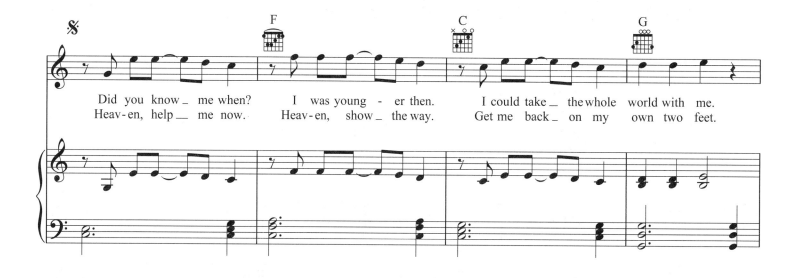

Did you know _ me when?   I was young - er then.   I could take _ the whole world with me.
Heav-en, help _ me now.   Heav-en, show _ the way.   Get me back _ on my own two feet.

I would find _ my-self   feel-in' a - lone, _   oh. _____
I would lie _ a-wake   and pray _ you don't   lie   a-wake   for me. __

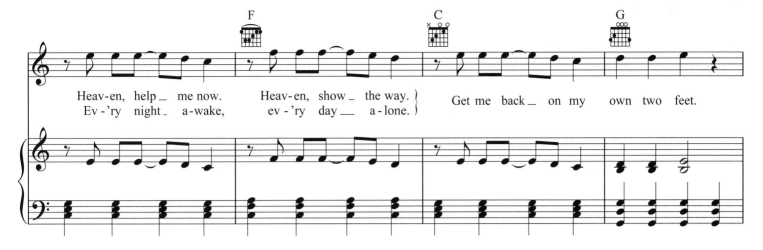

Heav-en, help me now. Heav-en, show the way.
Ev-'ry night a-wake, ev-'ry day a-lone. Get me back on my own two feet.

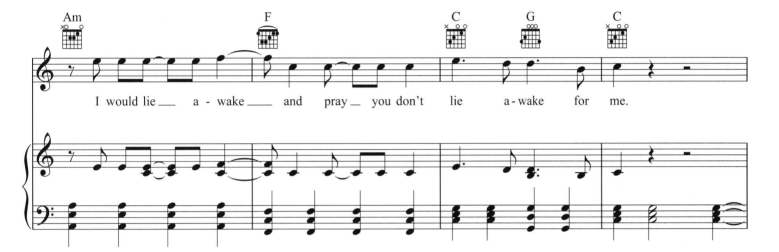

I would lie a - wake and pray you don't lie a-wake for me.

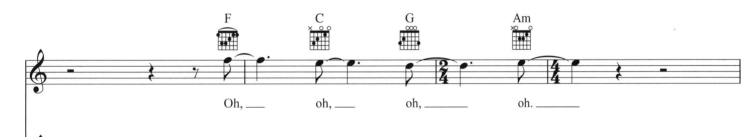

Oh, oh, oh, oh.

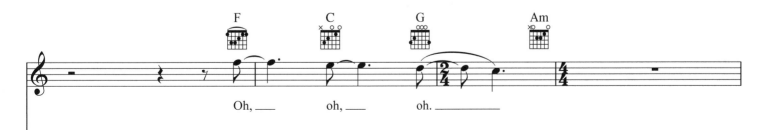

Oh, oh, oh.

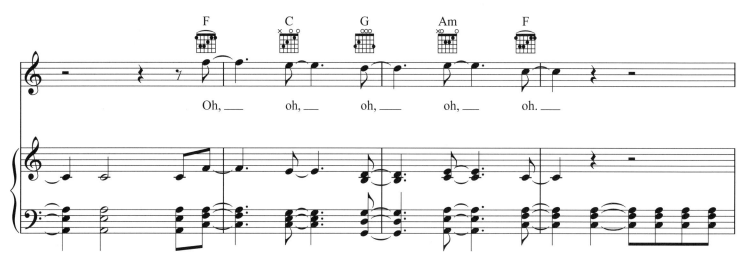

Oh, __ oh, __ oh, __ oh, __ oh. __

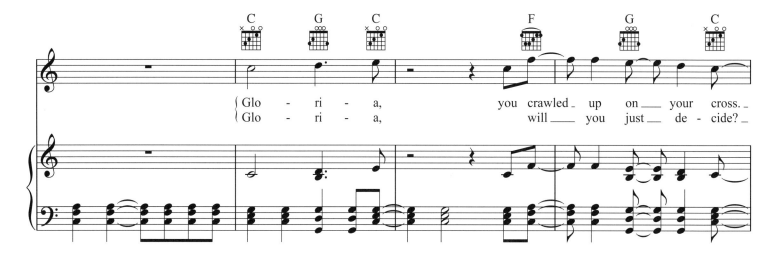

Glo - ri - a, you crawled __ up on __ your cross. __
Glo - ri - a, will __ you just __ de - cide? __

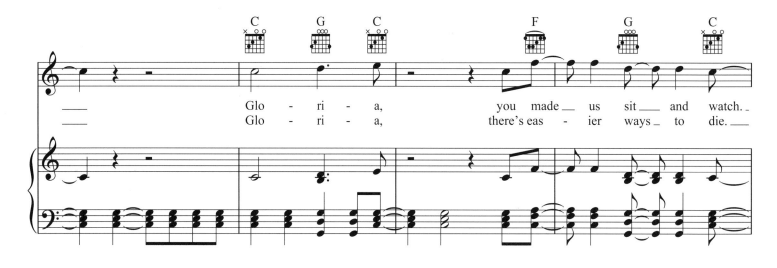

__ Glo - ri - a, you made __ us sit __ and watch. __
__ Glo - ri - a, there's eas - ier ways __ to die. __

__ Glo - ri - a, __ no __ one said __ e - nough __
__ Glo - ri - a, __ have __ you had __ e - nough? __

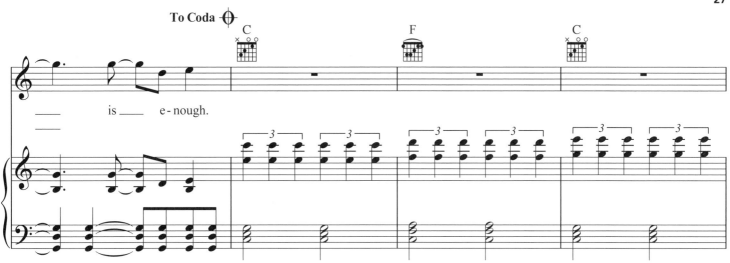

is ___ e - nough.

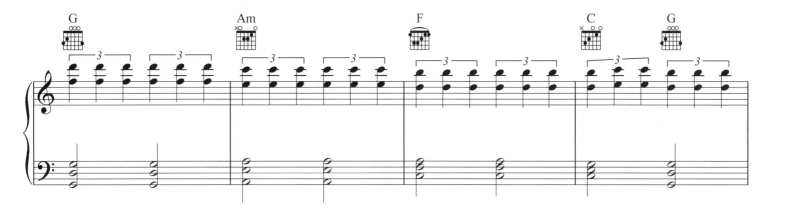

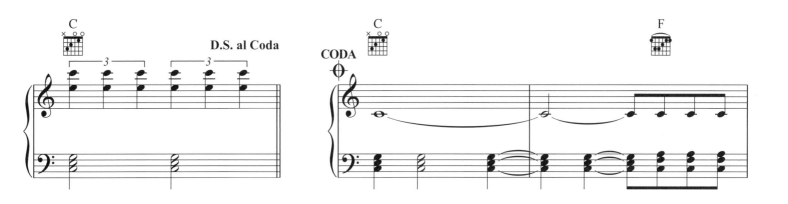

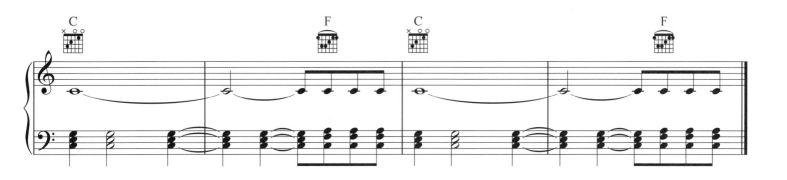

IT WASN'T EASY TO BE HAPPY FOR YOU

Words and Music by JEREMY FRAITES
and WESLEY SCHULTZ

shut me out, spilled my blood all a-round.
now you sleep on your own. Guess we'll see.

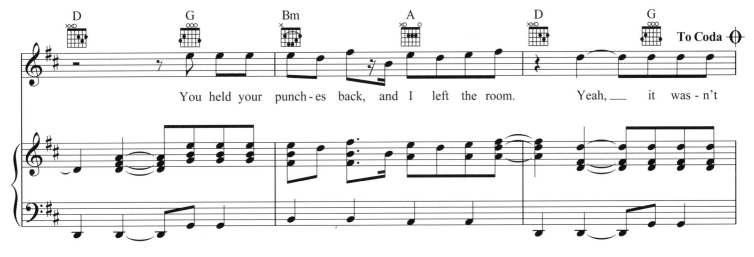

Yeah, it was-n't eas-y to be hap-py for you. Yeah, I took the poi-son pray-ing you'd feel it too.

You held your punch-es back, and I left the room. Yeah, it was-n't

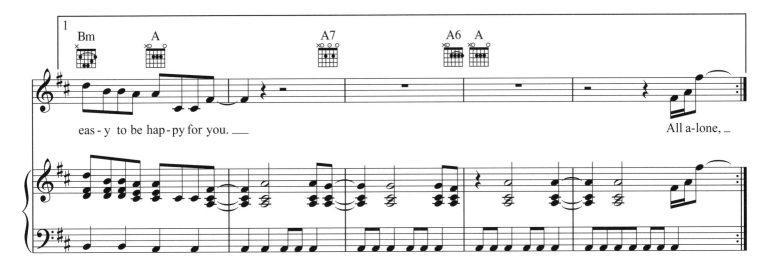

eas-y to be hap-py for you. All a-lone,

easy to be happy for you. I know that you tried, But you're no friend of mine.

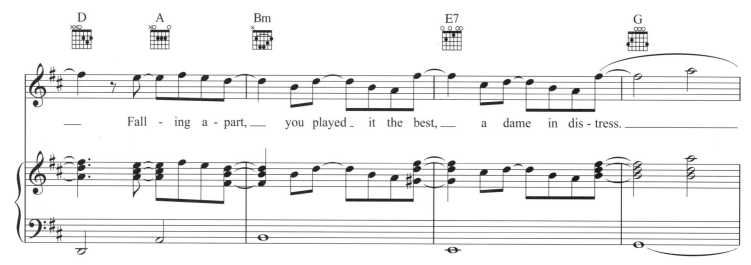

Falling apart, you played it the best, a dame in distress.

Yeah, it wasn't easy to be happy for you. Yeah, I wrapped my

neck and prayed that you'd feel the noose. I saw the restaurant table for two.

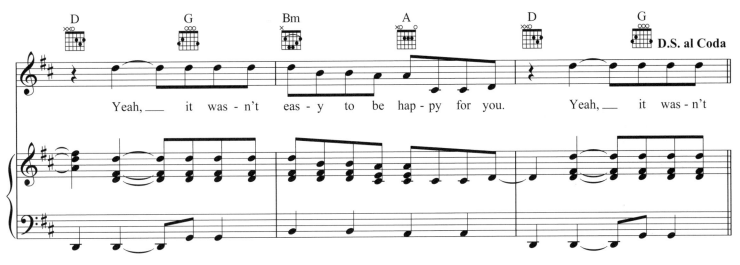

D.S. al Coda

Yeah, ___ it was-n't eas-y to be hap-py for you. Yeah, ___ it was-n't

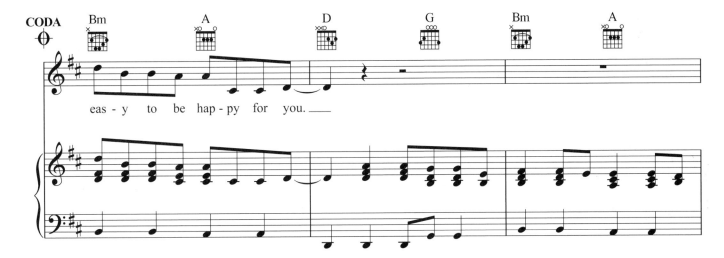

CODA

eas-y to be hap-py for you. ___

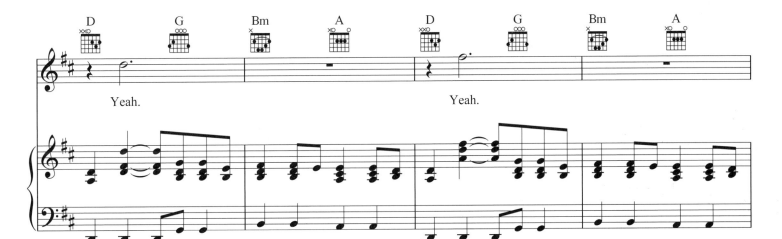

Yeah.   Yeah.

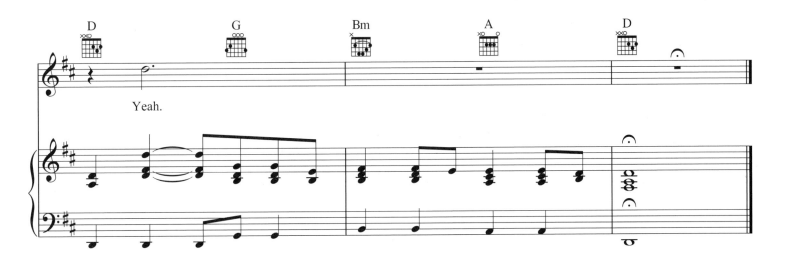

Yeah.

LEADER OF THE LANDSLIDE

Words and Music by JEREMY FRAITES
and WESLEY SCHULTZ

Ev-'ry night, I saw you there ___ in your old wick-er chair, ___ sing-ing,
Cof-fee mug, ___ filled it up. ___ Al-ways knew what it was. ___ Sing, ___

no. ___
no. ___

You were wrong, I ___ was right; did-n't mat-ter in a fight. Said,
Been on your side ___ for years. You could nev-er love ___ with-out cry'n'.

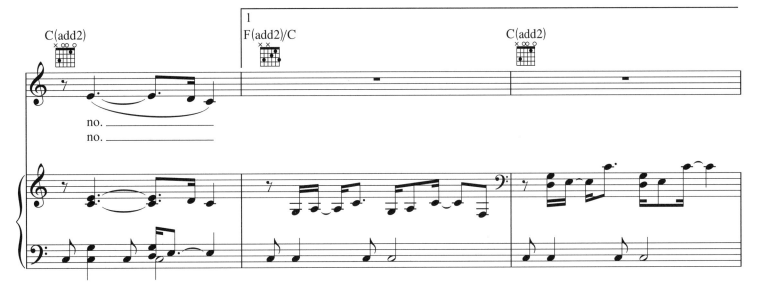

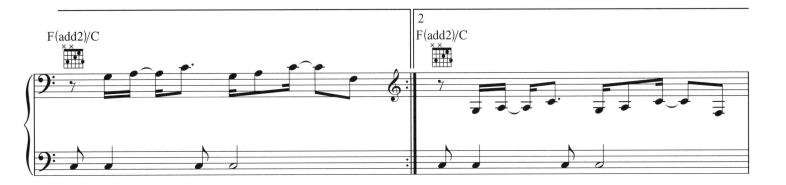

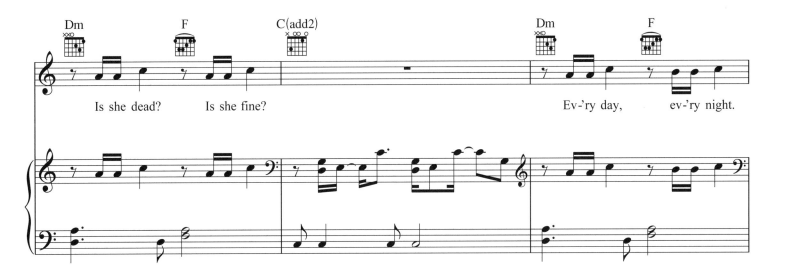

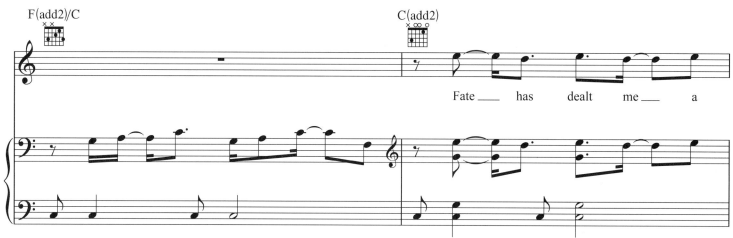

Fate ___ has dealt me ___ a

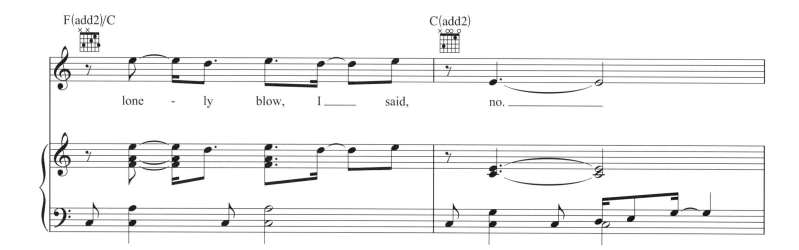

lone - ly blow, I ___ said, no. ___

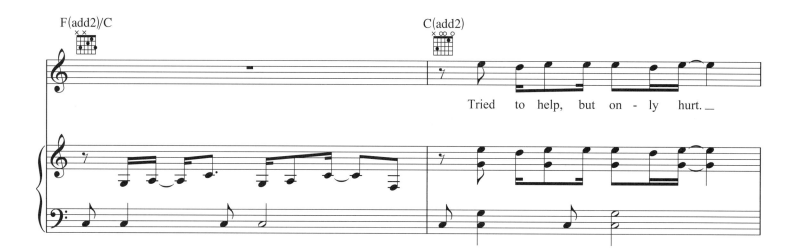

Tried to help, but on - ly hurt. ___

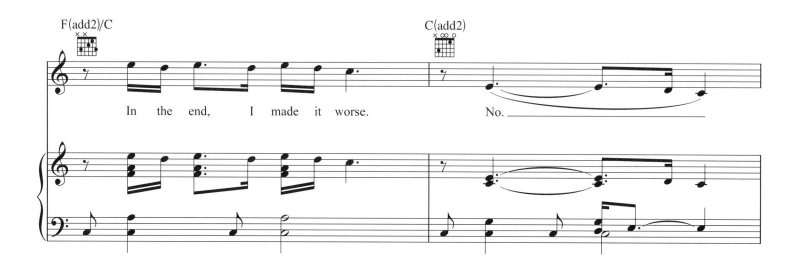

In the end, I made it worse. No. ___

Is she dead? Is she fine?

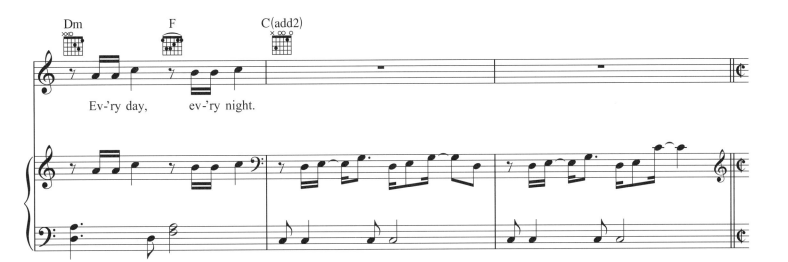

Ev-'ry day, ev-'ry night.

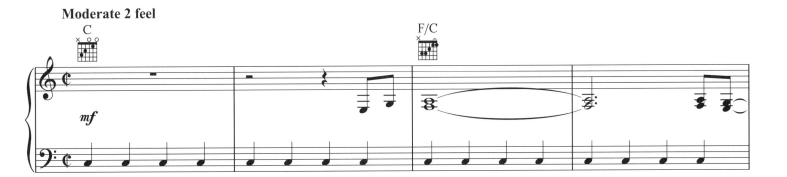

Moderate 2 feel

mf

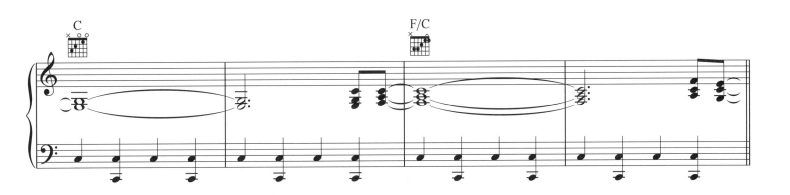

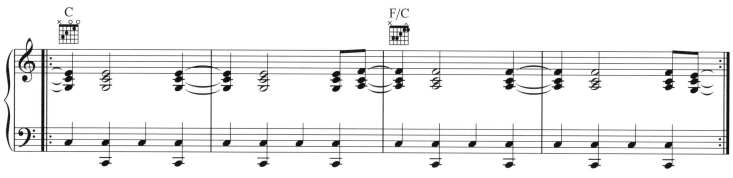

Give back my keys, give back my chair, take back those

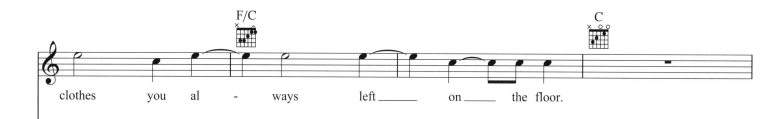

clothes you al - ways left _____ on _____ the floor.

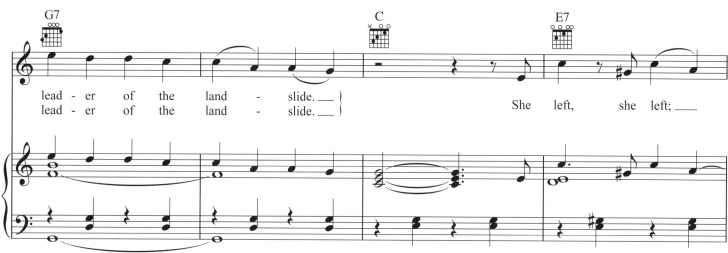

lead - er of the land - slide. ___ }
lead - er of the land - slide. ___ }

She left, she left; ___

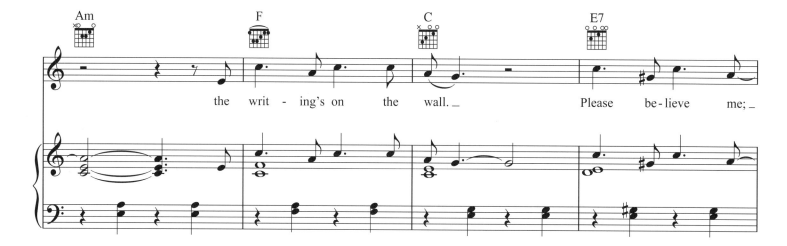

the writ - ing's on the wall. ___ Please be - lieve me; ___

___ { I smell the al - co - hol. }
{ don't an - swer when she calls. }

The on - ly thing ___ I

know is that we're in too deep, ___ and may - be when ___ she's

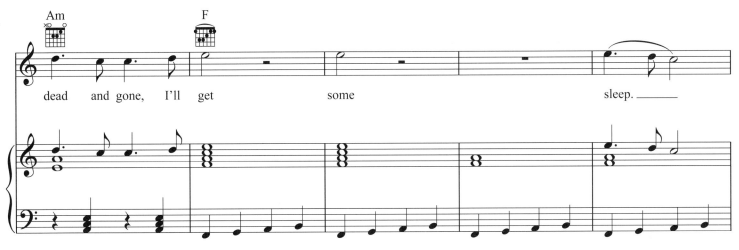

dead and gone, I'll get some sleep. _____

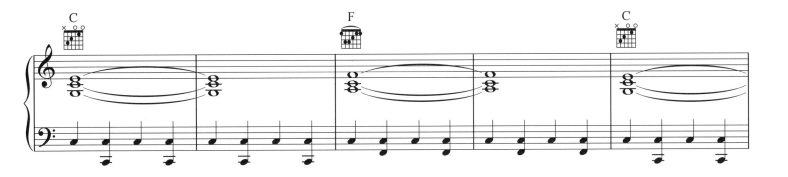

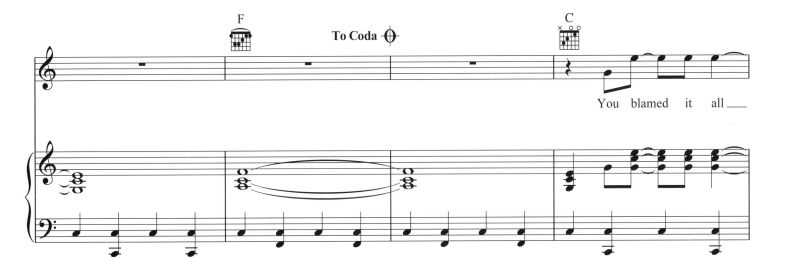

You blamed it all _____

on _____ your kids. _____ We were young, _

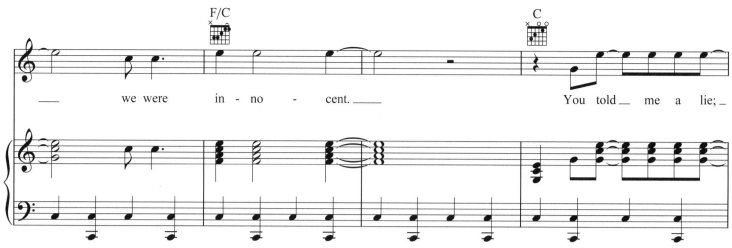

we were in - no - cent. ___ You told ___ me a lie; ___

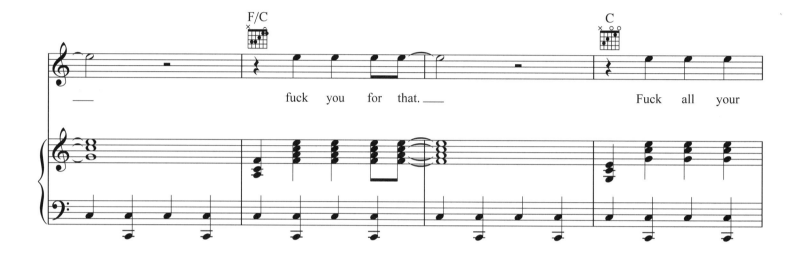

fuck you for that. ___ Fuck all your

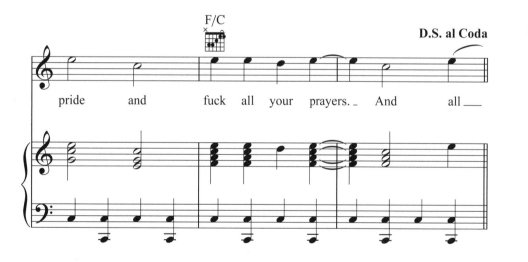

pride and fuck all your prayers. ___ And all ___

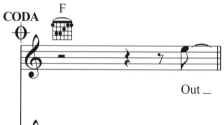

Out ___

___ there on my own, _____ I was feel - ing so a - lone, ___ like a pol -
- ing by de - grees, _____ I was shak - ing in the knees ___ in the af -

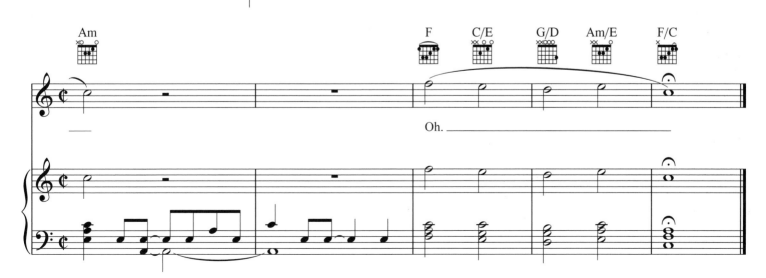

LEFT FOR DENVER

Words and Music by JEREMY FRAITES
and WESLEY SCHULTZ

Moderately slow

With pedal

What time _ was it __ when you _ were on - ly eight - een _ years _ old?

You crossed _ the street, _ you crossed _ your legs, ___ you came _ a-cross _ a lit-tle cold. _

And it was all, ___ it was all, _

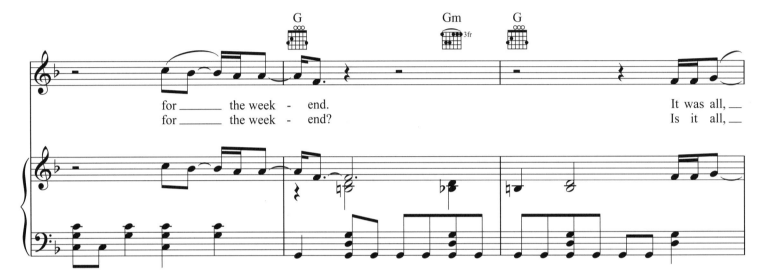

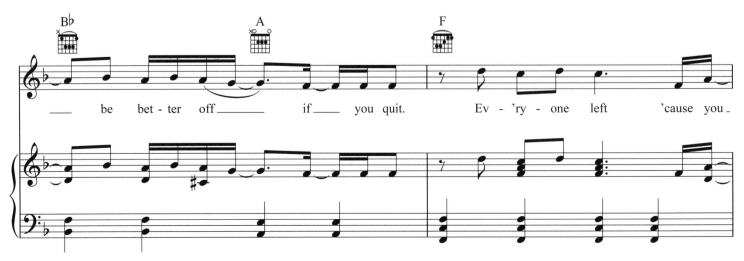

held on long - er than __ the rest. What made you leave? And when you did, __

__ you left __ for Den - ver. __ Why? ___ What did you know that I __

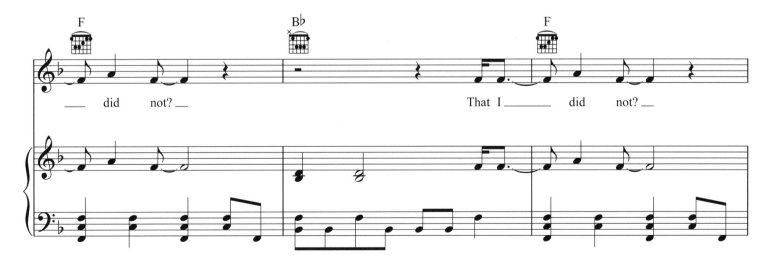

__ did not? __ That I _____ did not? __

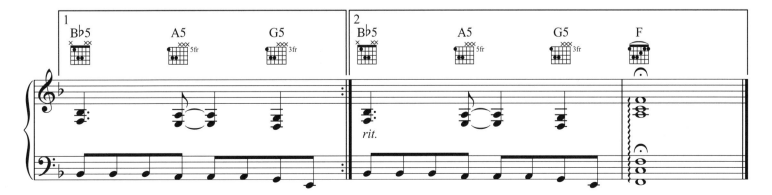

MY CELL

Words and Music by JEREMY FRAITES
and WESLEY SCHULTZ

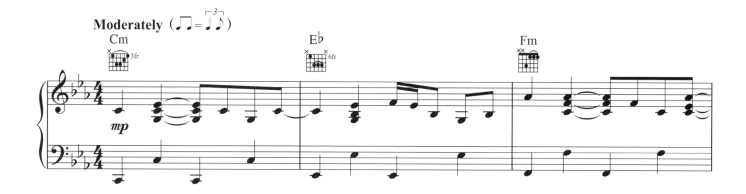

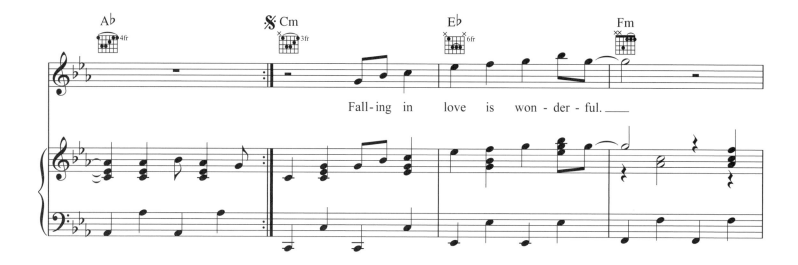

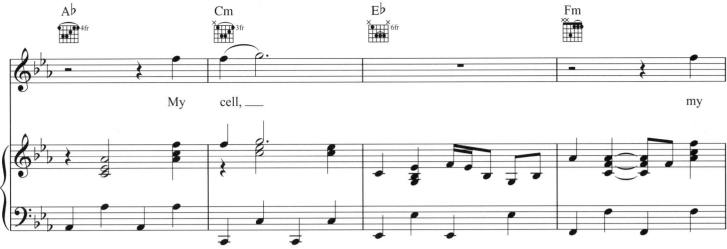

My cell, ___ my

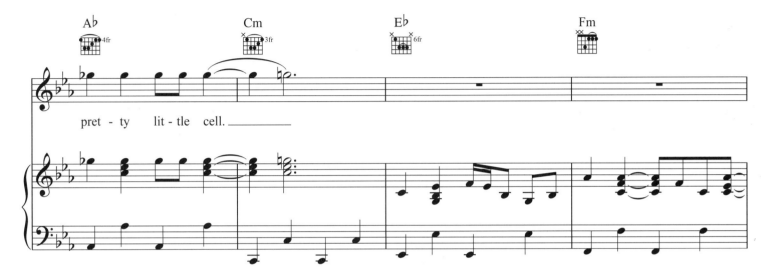

pret - ty lit - tle cell. _____

Pain-ted win - dows _____ there for me. ___
Pain-ted win - dows _____ so I see. ___

To Coda ⊕

Pain-ted win - dows _____ so I can see. _____
Pain-ted win - dows _____ all ___ for me. _____

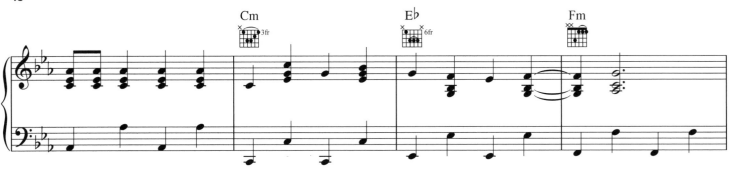

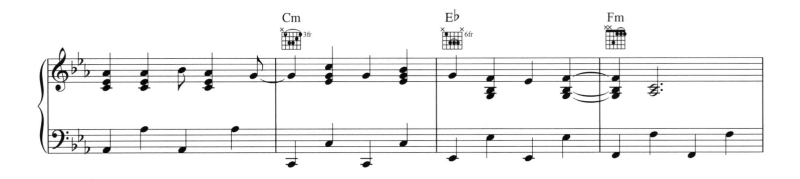

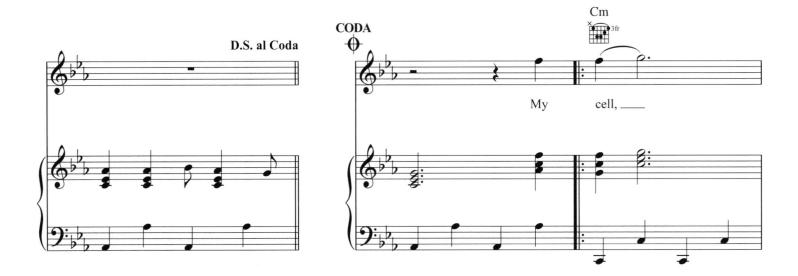

APRIL

Words and Music by JEREMY FRAITES
and WESLEY SCHULTZ

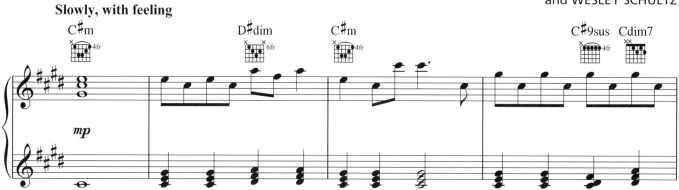

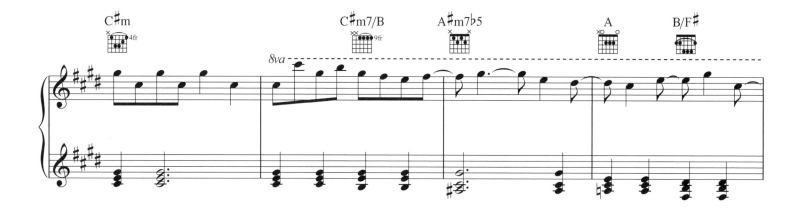

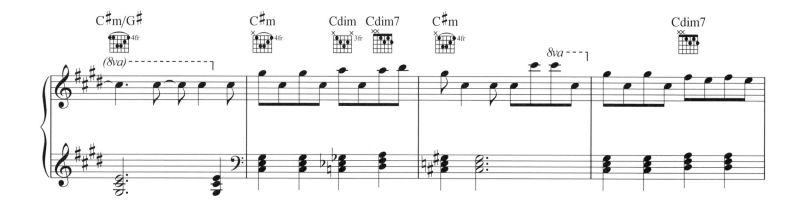

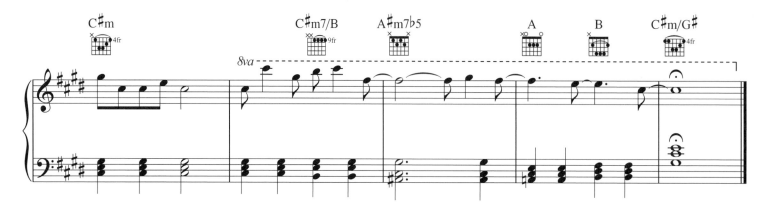

OLD LADY

Words and Music by JEREMY FRAITES
and WESLEY SCHULTZ

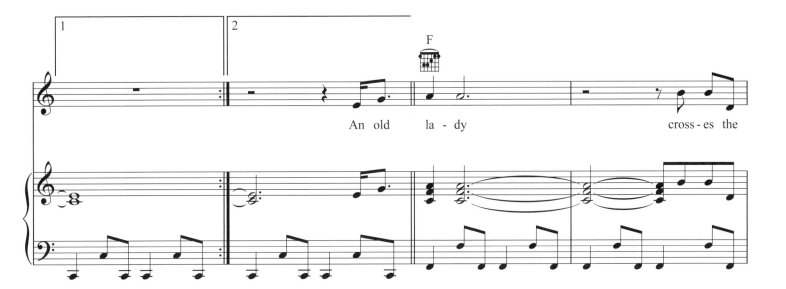

An old la-dy cross-es the

street. ___ And as she waves to me ___ I don't

see her.   And I know that one day I.

Ooh, _____

ooh. _____   Ooh, _____

ooh. _____

To Coda ⊕

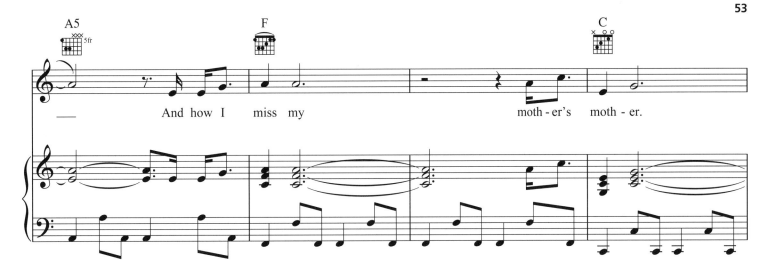

And how I miss my moth-er's moth-er.

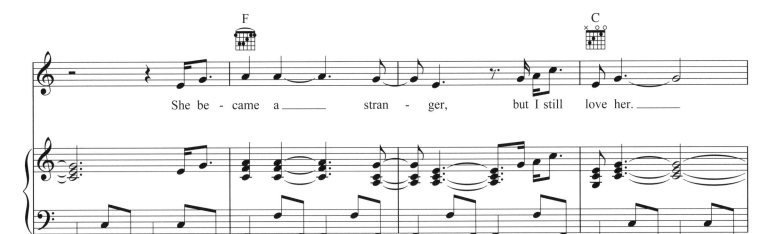

She be-came a _____ stran - ger, but I still love her. _____

And I hope, I hope she turns.

D.S. al Coda

Ooh, __

CODA

__ Now the day __ came,

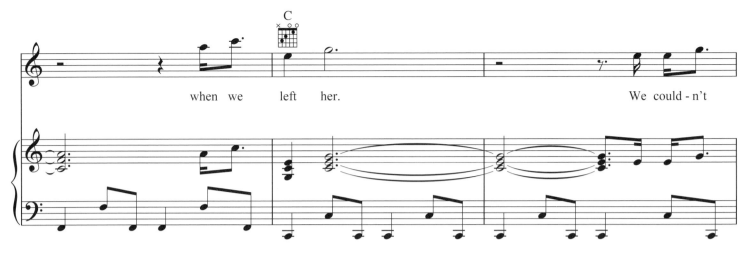

when we left her. We could-n't

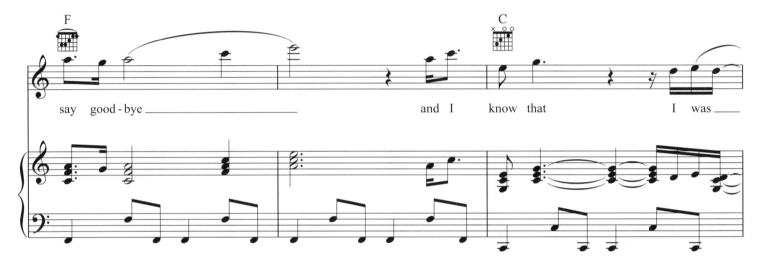

say good-bye _____ and I know that I was _____

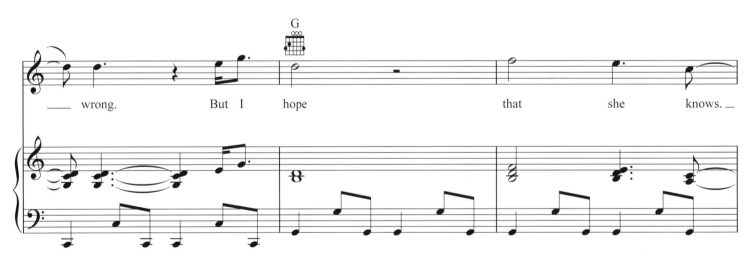

_____ wrong. But I hope that she knows. _____

Ooh, _____

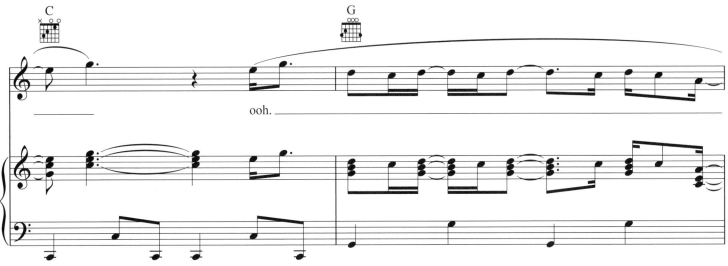

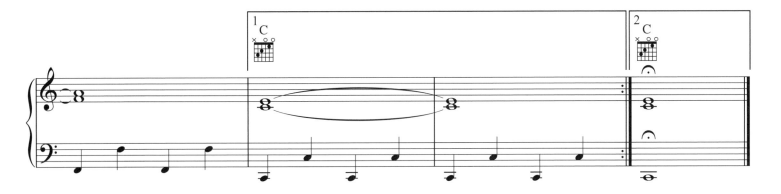

SALT AND THE SEA

Words and Music by JEREMY FRAITES
and WESLEY SCHULTZ

- case you fell __ to your knees __ with tears __ in your eyes. __

All that you suf - fer'd, all the dis - ease. __ You could-n't __ hide __

__ it, hide it from me. __ All a-lone scared __ in your room __ would you swear __
__ these pre-scrip - tions, they wrote __

__ there's no - bod - y home? __ On the bed lay -
__ me off __ like a heel. __ Yeah, the doc - tors __

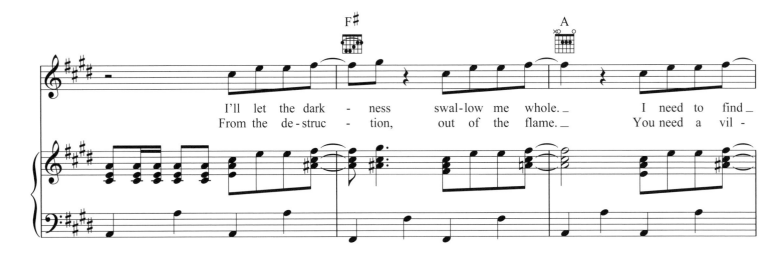

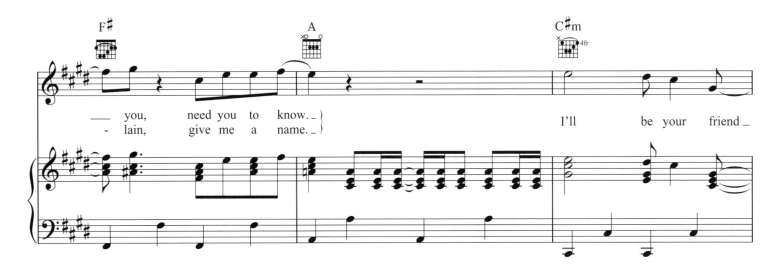

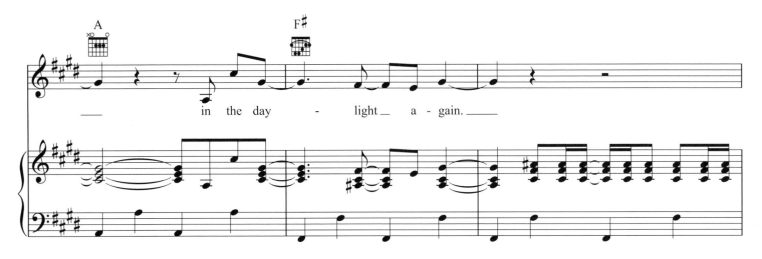

There we will be ____ like an old ____ en - e - my. ____

____ Like the salt ____ and ____ the sea. ____

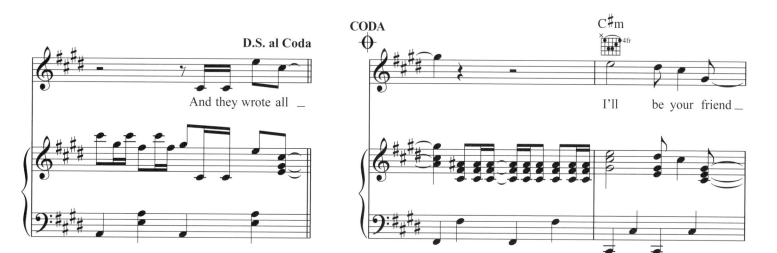

And they wrote all _

I'll be your friend _

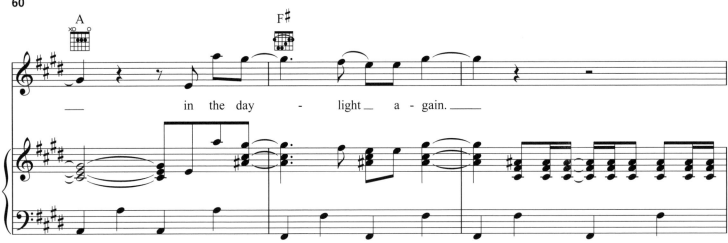

in the day - light ___ a - gain. ___

There we will be ___ like an old ___ en - e - my.

___ Like the salt ___ and ___ the sea. ___ Like the salt ___

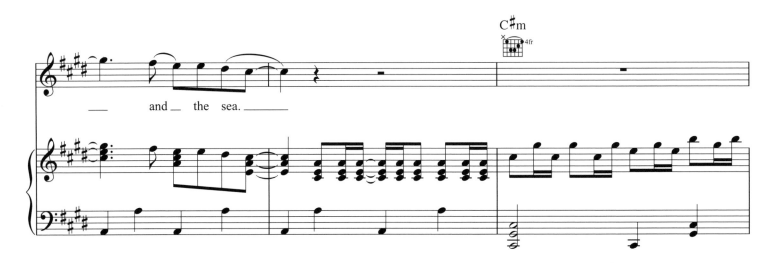

___ and ___ the sea. ___

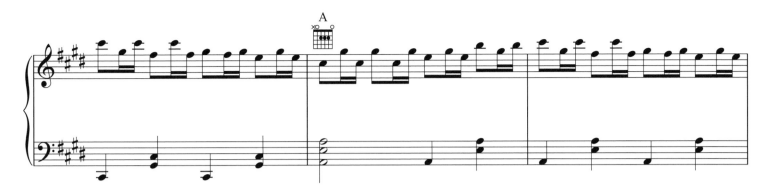

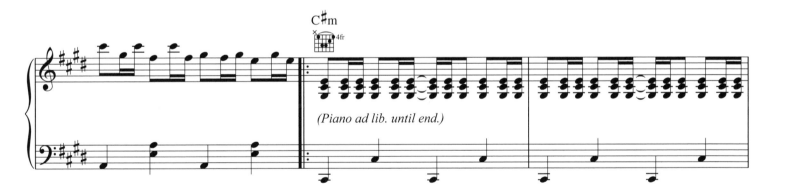

(Piano ad lib. until end.)

Play 3 times

DEMOCRACY

Words and Music by JEREMY FRAITES
and WESLEY SCHULTZ

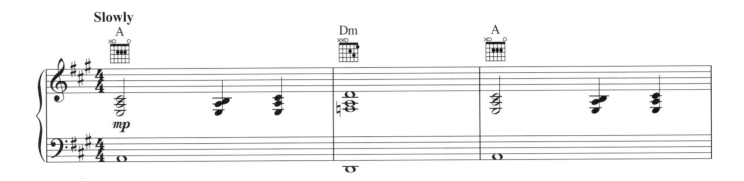

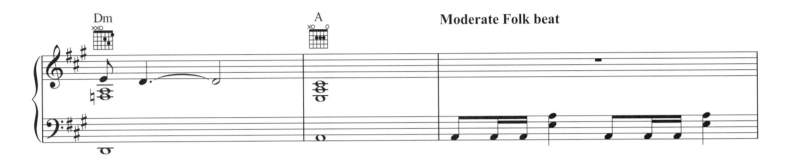

It's com-

-in   through a hole _____ in the air _____   from those ___
com-in' through a   crack _____ in the wall ___   on a
com-in' from the   sor row _____ in the streets, _   the ho-

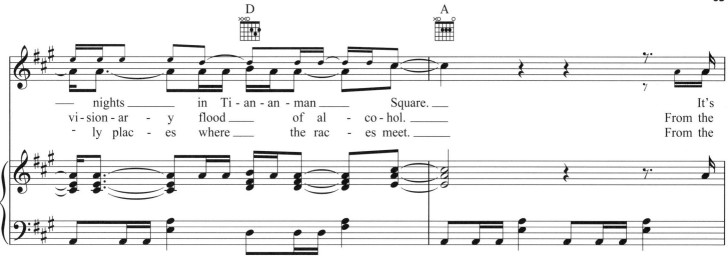

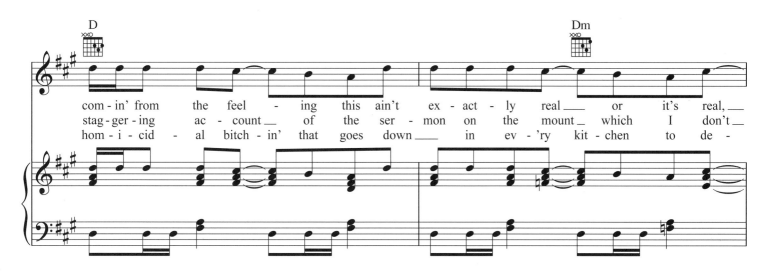

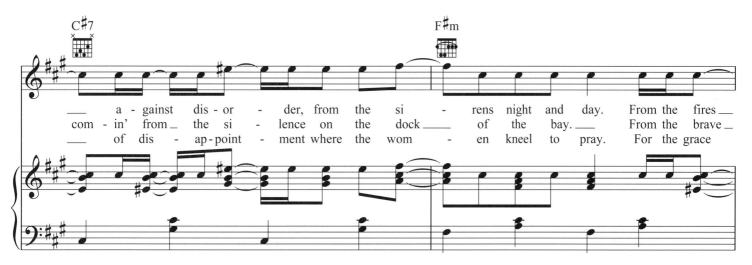

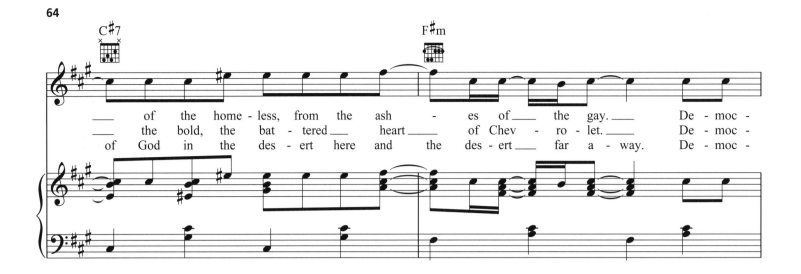

of the home-less, from the ash-es of___ the gay.___ De-moc-
the bold, the bat-tered___ heart___ of Chev-ro-let.___ De-moc-
of God in the des-ert here and the des-ert___ far a-way.___ De-moc-

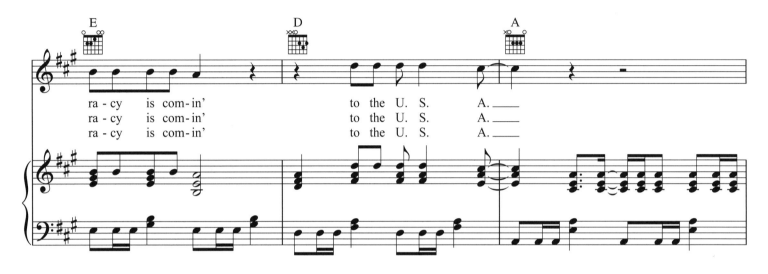

ra-cy is com-in' to the U. S. A.___
ra-cy is com-in' to the U. S. A.___
ra-cy is com-in' to the U. S. A.___

It's Sail on,___ sail on_
It's

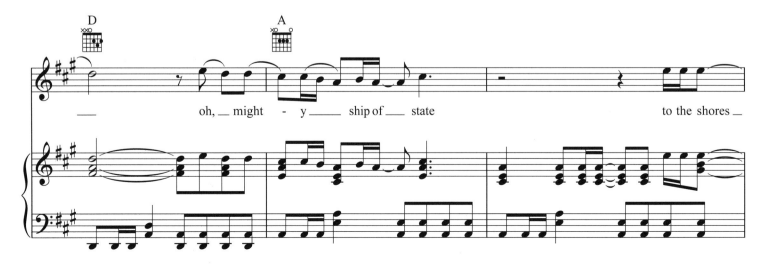

___ oh, ___ might-y___ ship of ___ state to the shores ___

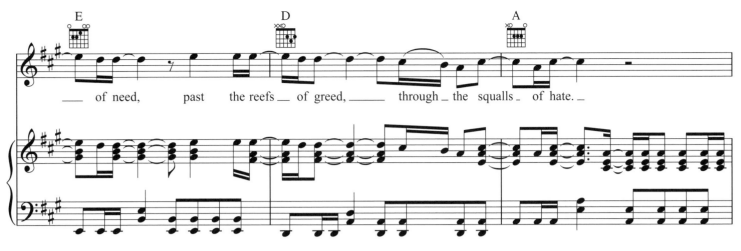

of need, past the reefs __ of greed, _____ through _ the squalls _ of hate. __

Sail on, ____ sail on, ____ sail on. __

To Coda

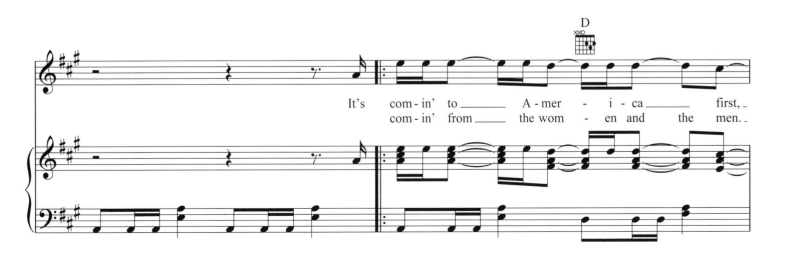

It's com - in' to _____ A - mer - i - ca _____ first, __

com - in' from _____ the wom - en and the men. __

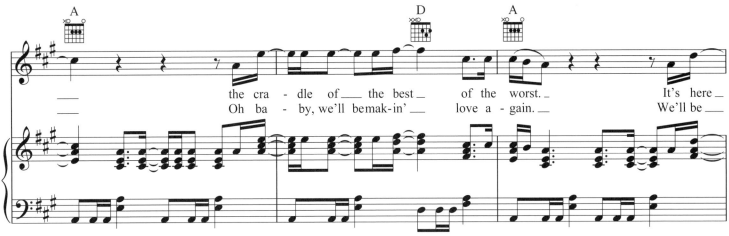

the cra - dle of __ the best __ of the worst. _ It's here __
Oh ba - by, we'll be mak-in' __ love a - gain. _ We'll be __

__ they've got __ the range __ and the __ ma-chin - er - y for change _ and it's here __
__ go - in' down so __ deep that __ the riv - er's gon - na weep __ and the moun -

__ they've got __ the spir - it - u - al thirst. __ It's
- tain's gon - na shout, "A - men." __ It's

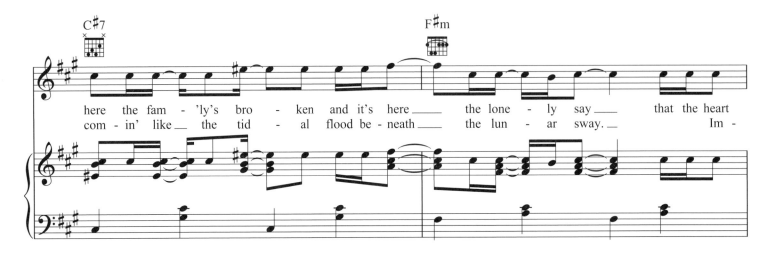

here the fam - 'ly's bro - ken and it's here ___ the lone - ly say __ that the heart
com - in' like __ the tid - al flood be - neath __ the lun - ar sway. __ Im -

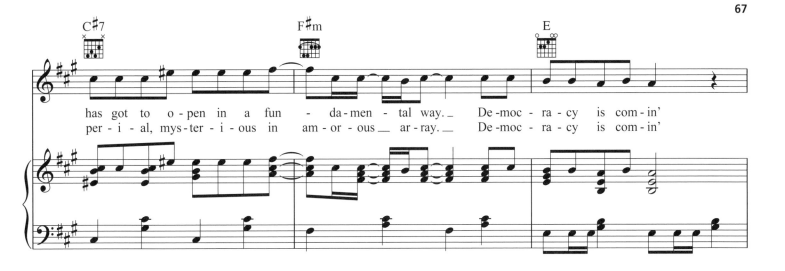

has got to o-pen in a fun - da-men - tal way._ De-moc-ra-cy is com-in'
per - i - al, mys-ter - i - ous in am-or-ous_ ar - ray._ De-moc-ra-cy is com-in'

to the U. S. A. ___
to the U. S. A. ___

It's

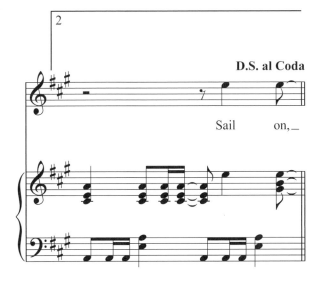

D.S. al Coda

Sail on, _

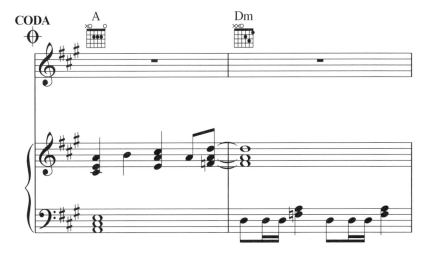

CODA

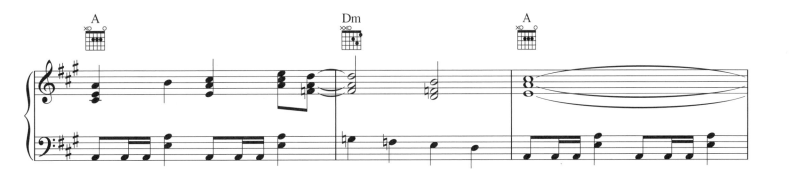

I'm sen-ti-men-tal, if you know what I mean. _ Oh, I love _

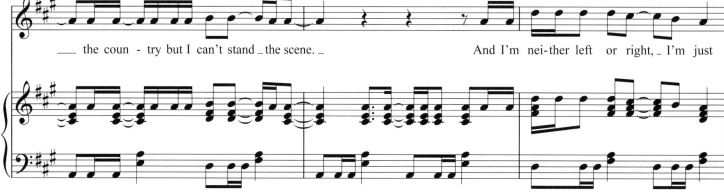

___ the coun-try but I can't stand _ the scene. _ And I'm nei-ther left or right, _ I'm just

stay-in' home _ to-night _ get-tin' lost ___ in that hope-less lit-tle ___ screen. _ But I'm stub-

- born as those gar-bage bags that time ___ can-not _ de-cay. _ I'm junk, _ but I'm still hold-in' up this

SOUNDTRACK SONG

Words and Music by JEREMY FRAITES
and WESLEY SCHULTZ

Lone-li-ness, _ oh, won't you let me be? Let me be _ and I will

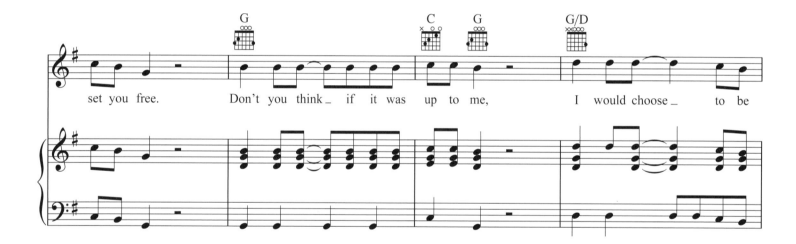

set you free. Don't you think _ if it was up to me, I would choose _ to be

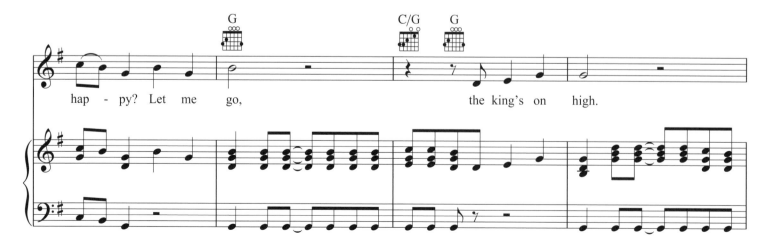

hap-py? Let me go, the king's on high.

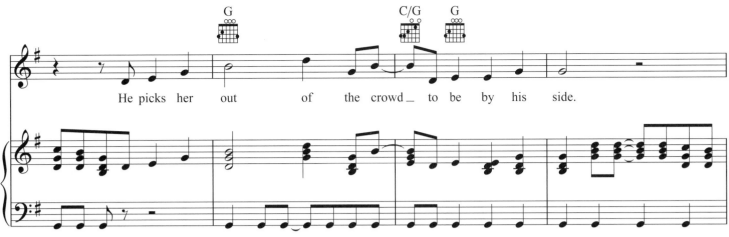

He picks her out of the crowd __ to be by his side.

She walks up, stair - case in white.

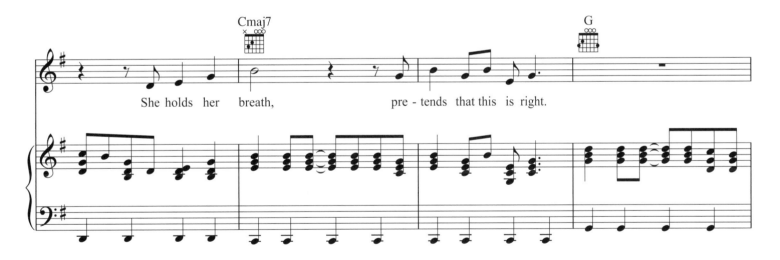

She holds her breath, pre - tends that this is right.

'Cause all of this, __ it don't __ come free. __ And don't __ be - come __ a cas -
cow - ards and __ he - roes feel __ the same __ as you __ and me, __
vic - to - ry __ is in __ the fight. __ In men __ with hearts __ that bleed __

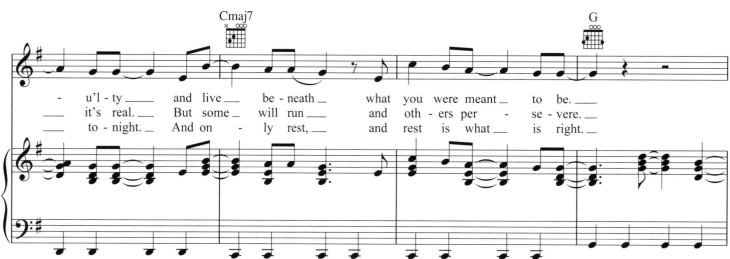

- u'l - ty ____ and live ____ be - neath ____ what you were meant ___ to be. ____
____ it's real. ___ But some ____ will run ___ and oth - ers per - se - vere. ____
____ to - night. ___ And on - ly rest, ___ and rest is what ___ is right. ____

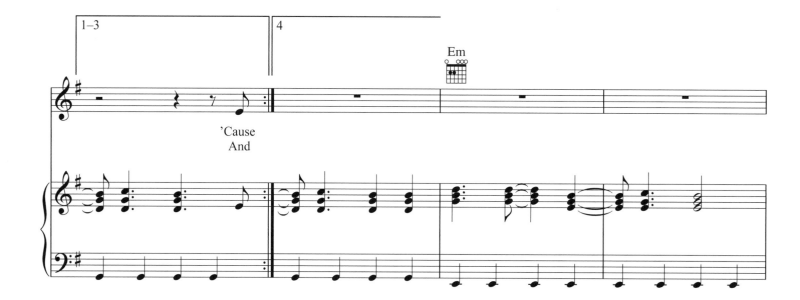

'Cause
And

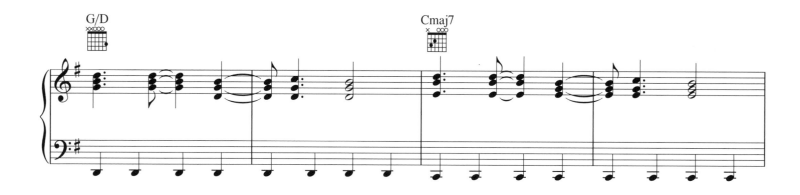

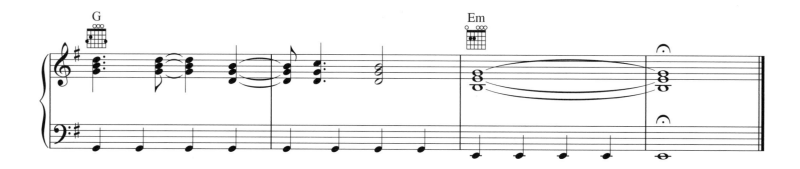